"This book is written with the firm conviction that how we respond to life's great questions is important." This author doesn't preach, shame, or push an agenda. He truly cares about the family relationship and is offering hope and practical ways to address reality.

Rev. Shauna Hyde
Pastor, First UMC, Ravenswood, WV
Author of *Vicar of Tent Town*

PRAISE FOR *A HOME UNITED*

A Home United by Bob LaRochelle provides a pathway for couples of different faiths to explore the implications of their religious differences and to deal with them in constructive and fulfilling ways. Bob's personal religious journey, from a Roman Catholic communicant to an ordained United Church of Christ minister, provides him with both the theological and practical perspective to be helpful to the bi-faith couple. While Bob shares insights gained from his own experience, the pathway he shares is lined with questions rather than answers. As he points out, each couple's answers will be unique. His book and the questions he asks therein are provided to help couples examine their religious differences and create their own answers. As a clinical psychologist, I often dealt with the marital train after it had gone off the tracks, trying to repair the damage done to the couple, their children, and their families. I would see Bob's book as an important adjunct to pre-marital counseling or a great engagement gift. Marriage is perhaps the most important contract people sign – *A Home United* encourages and assists the couple to read the fine print.

Curtis Brand, PhD, Psychologist,
Author and music man, curtisbrand.com

A slim volume filled with helpful discussion questions, *A Home United* should spark important conversations for both couples and congregations, as we move together into a more religiously plural country. Bob LaRochelle, a progressive Protestant minister married to a Catholic woman, wrestles with the challenges and affirms the benefits of interfaith families in a way that will be particularly helpful to Christians. But every couple, even those who share a religious denomination, could benefit from tackling LaRochelle's philosophical, theological and practical questions about how to live together across religious differences.

Susan Katz Miller
Author of *Being Both: Embracing Two Religions in One Interfaith Family*

In *A Home United*, Rev. Dr. Bob LaRochelle uses his unique perspective to help guide couples through the conflicts that can accompany differing religious beliefs. While reading this book, I found myself not only more closely examining the beliefs of my wife, but re-identifying my own spiritual conclusions. The material is presented not as a lecture, but rather a conversation. I would recommend *A Home United* as a valuable study guide for couples at any stage of their relationship. Rev. LaRochelle speaks from the heart, using his own real-world experiences to illuminate the challenges and rewards of an interfaith relationship.

Eric R. Hutchinson, Songwriter/Composer
(*Lullabies and Love Songs, Melt, Still, Believer: The Musical*,
Imagine Stage Productions)

What you want from any author who proposes to help you sort out your own life is one who has overcome the very challenges you face. Bob LaRochelle is such an author if you find yourself in a mixed-faith marriage with its attendant issues. More than a book (descriptive), it offers solid help, not by providing simple answers, but by showing you the questions that will lead you to your own solutions. Equally valuable for those contemplating marriage and those already married. A must for religious leaders of all faiths.

Rev. Steven F. Kindle,
Executive Director of *Clergy United*,
author of *I'm Right And You're Wrong* and *Stewardship: God's Way of Recreating the World*, Lake Shasta, CA

I love it when someone notices a current social dynamic and offers a usable resource! LaRochelle has put together a book that can be used in counseling (before and after a wedding), in a small group study, and in the home. He has honestly, yet delicately, offered the truth about religion and relationships and a way to address that truth. In a world of melded and blended families this book is written to truly help them blend beautifully. LaRochelle writes,

A

HOME

UNITED

A PARTICIPATORY STUDY GUIDE

STRATEGIES FOR COUPLES WITH DIFFERENT BELIEFS

ROBERT R. LAROCHELLE

Energion Publications
Gonzalez, FL
2015

Cover Image: ID 26205181 © Nvnkarthik| Dreamstime.com

Cover Design: Henry Neufeld

ISBN10: 1-63199-181-7
ISBN13: 978-1-63199-181-3
Library of Congress Control Number: 2015945368

Energion Publications
P. O. Box 841
Gonzalez, FL 32560

Web: energion.com
E-mail: pubs@energion.com
850-525-3916

Acknowledgments

This book has been greatly influenced by so many people who have helped to shape my understanding of the wide variety of human religious experience. This includes so many of my teachers as well as those who, over the years, have shared their own personal stories with me, often in my premarital preparation sessions with them. While there really are too many people to name, I wish to affirm my gratitude to all who have contributed to my understanding and awareness of the importance of what I would deem each person's own religious experience.

I am also deeply grateful to the many people who, by life, example, or words written, have pointed me in the direction of Jesus of Nazareth, the One whom I have freely chosen to seek to follow.

Robert R. LaRochelle
Lent 2015

THE PARTICIPATORY STUDY SERIES

The Participatory Study Series from Energion Publications is designed around the motto "scholarship in service." Each guide is written by someone with a strong background in the topic studied and designed for use by lay people in Sunday School classes and small groups, as well as for individual study.

These guides are not all easy reading. Some of the topics covered require serious effort on the part of the student. But the guides do provide all the resources necessary for a fruitful study.

The section "Using this Book" is designed for the series but adapted to the particular study guide. Each author is free to emphasize different resources in the study, and to follow his or her own plan in presenting the material.

It is our prayer at Energion Publications that each study guide will lead you to a deeper understanding of your Christian faith.

– Henry Neufeld, General Editor

USING THIS BOOK

This study guide is very helpful for small groups, such as Sunday School or adult education classes. Individual students working on their own will benefit from the stimulation it provides. It might serve as an introductory textbook.

The book itself will give you with an overview of a topic, marriage in homes with partners of different faiths, providing specific questions for discussion. There are several things you can do to make your study more profitable.

1. Where **resources** are suggested, divide them between members of the class and consult them during your study time. Students can bring what they have learned to the class. This is also a good time to help your church improve its library. Suggest some of these resources for your library shelves.

2. **Share.** The Participatory Study Guides to Bible books pioneered sharing as an integral part of your study, but it will work just as well when you are studying a topic. Sharing does not mean harassing other people with your viewpoint. It's a matter of listening and being accountable in your community. If you come to a conclusion, listen to others who can comment on it and possibly point out reasons that you may be wrong, or ideas that may not have occurred to you.

This is the third topical guide in this series. It is exceptionally practical. Be sure to think of living the word as you learn it!

TABLE OF CONTENTS

INTRODUCTION

I t is a well acknowledged fact that, since the 1960's, American religious institutions have undergone significant changes. Much has been written about the decline in attendance and personal affiliation and connection that most people have with local places of worship.[1] One of the areas that has changed considerably is the place that religious faith plays within our most significant and intimate human relationships. The days in which it was typical for couples to share a religious affiliation are, to a great extent, well behind us. All of the research indicates that for a large number of young adults, attendance at religious services is not part of their lives.[2] For many people in young adulthood, participation in religious activity was not even part of their childhood or adolescence. Whereas in previous generations, it was not uncommon for young adults to reject the faith of their childhood, in the current context, many young adults have simply not had a great deal of exposure to the tenets and practices of religious traditions. Likewise, couples with children are less likely than they once were to share the same religious perspective.

---

1   The Pew Center's Religion and Public Life project, in particular its Religious Landscape Survey, has been very helpful in providing relevant data. See http://religions.pewforum.org/ for a full exploration of a variety of religious trends in the United States. In my view, the data they have provided has been very helpful in describing the shifts in religious practice in American society. It should be noted that the study released in 2015 has shown a significant increase in the number of people who do not participate in activities associated with a religious institution, even if only occasionally.

2   While this varies somewhat by religious traditions, the data indicates that this trend is a significant contemporary reality and this has caught the attention of religious leaders.

Even in light of these significant demographic shifts, religious differences can have major impact upon interpersonal and family relationships. In fact, in many situations, they have helped to drive a chasm between individuals committed to one another as well as between them and members of their extended families. The purpose of this book is to suggest ways in which couples and families with different religious perspectives can confront these differences in positive ways which contribute to the nurturing of their relationships. This book will explore the multiple variations involved in real life religious situations and suggest approaches toward dealing with them in constructive and fulfilling ways.

I have written this with the intention that it will be applicable and relevant to couples in a wide variety of situations. Consequently, I would encourage you as you read this that you NOT envision these words as applying only to relationships involving heterosexual married couples. This book is intended to be meaningful to all couples who have chosen to forge a life together and who, in the process, must deal with religious matters as they affect their relationship.

I say this all at the beginning of this book recognizing that some who would opt to read this book will look at couples in the way I just described. They would see the lessons found in this book to be applicable to married heterosexual couples alone. I would contend that even if a reader is troubled by my assertion that its applicability is more general than one might desire, it is important that individuals understand my purpose. This book is **not** intended only for heterosexual couples who are married or considering marriage nor is it a book about what one considers to be normative and traditional in committed relationships. In saying this, I wish to be clear upfront that I do not shy away from my support of marriage equality. In fact, all of the current evidence shows that American society has undergone significant shifts in this area.[3] What is also

3   In the years 2014-15, during the writing of this book, an increasing number of states have legalized marriage between same sex couples and polls have

clear is that those issues in the area of religious difference which affect heterosexual couples affect homosexual couples as well. This includes concerns involving the religious upbringing of children. My hope is that if you, the reader, share a different perspective from mine, you will not look unfavorably at the value of what I am writing because of this difference in opinion.

Ideally, this book is intended to be a resource for couples in the situations I describe within it. In addition, it can serve as a resource book for those within congregations who work with these couples. It might even be of value to those, including clergy and all pastoral leaders, who are considering how church religious communities might respond to the changing demographics that have led to the need for such a resource.

As we begin this exploration, it is important that I tell you something about myself. I write this book as a pastor in a Protestant Christian church. I was raised and spent the first forty five years of my life as a member of the Roman Catholic Church. Ordained in and an authorized minister within the United Church of Christ, I am currently serving as a pastor in a congregation of the Evangelical Lutheran Church of America.[4] I have been married to a Roman Catholic woman for almost thirty five years at the time of this book's release and our three children are Catholic as well, though each individually has her/his own perspective on theological and ecclesiastical matters. Over the course of my pastoral ministry, I have spent considerable time and effort working with couples in inter-denominational and interfaith situations. In addition, I have done premarital preparation with individuals who have had very little

indicated growing public acceptance. On June 26, 2015, just prior to this book's publication, the United States Supreme Court ruled in favor of marriage equality in all fifty states.

4   This is possible because of the *Formula of Agreement* among several churches, an important ecumenical agreement in the life of American Protestantism. This ecumenical agreement includes the Presbyterian Church USA, the United Church of Christ, the Reformed Church in America and the Evangelical Lutheran Church in America.

connection with organized religion. Likewise, I have worked with with couples in a wide variety of situations in celebrating religious rituals for their children. While I am a Christian by conviction and affirmation of faith, I also contend that God speaks and acts through a multiplicity of different ways, both within and outside the Christian church. In saying this, I am trying to be as transparent as possible to the reader, realizing fully well that some Christians more conservative than I might find my position problematic.

In addition, I also find myself considerably troubled that the pluralism of religious approach[5] among couples has led many to take the 'safe' route in which advocating no religious approach is considered the best alternative as a way of insuring minimum relational tension. My concern here is that the discussion of religion has, in all too many cases, been omitted from conversations between couples and within families. This religious neutrality, while intended to promote unity, might instead produce the effect of depriving couples and families of important life experiences and of sharing worthwhile conversations. In many cases, it may also provide fertile ground for pent up or expressed resentments between individuals and within extended families. As a result of this religious neutrality, individuals may be deprived of many rich benefits that come from a healthy exploration of the variety of religious ideas and practices which may exist within their own familial context.

Of course, religious pluralism in close relationships carries with it the capacity to be explosive. It has been and can be the cause of tense intrafamilial and interrelational disputes. It can get particularly nasty when it comes to issues related to the raising of children. Many individuals who have lived in interreligious homes can tell real horror stories. This book is intended to provide alterna-

---

5 The use of the phrase 'religious approach' is intentional and is defined specifically in Chapter Three. It encompasses more than affiliation with a particular organized religion, e.g. Catholicism. It takes into account the reality that with respect to important life questions, all human beings have opinions that shape their lives.

tive, positive ways to deal with these potential areas of discord. It is based on the premise that the depth and quality of one's relationship with a spouse, partner or child is not dependent on whether you might share the same specific theological perspectives and/or definable religious world view.

I say all this with a full recognition that human relationships **are** based on points of connection and shared beliefs. I am hopeful that this will be clear as we move through this book. As people engage in a healthy, positive open sharing of religious perspectives, they may even surprise themselves with how and where they find what they have in common. It is my goal in this book to help that happen.

It is important that I say from the beginning that for the approach I suggest in this book to work within relationships, each individual must have an openness to the reality that those with different religious perspectives should not simply be "converted to the truth." In other words those who approach the matter of religious faith with this mindset might impede the possibilities to be found in ongoing, healthy, shared dialogue.

If one, as an example, were a fundamentalist Christian who would believe that unless his agnostic wife accepts Jesus as Savior, she would some day be burning in hell, I think it is fair to say that this attitude might very well have a negative effect on the relationship. It is my hope that you, the reader, might find this an interesting topic to explore and discuss with others who are exposed to this book.

In an attempt to help you delve into the important issues surrounding this topic, I have structured what you are about to read in this manner: Chapter One will look at the changed reality of religious life among couples and within families over the course of the late twentieth and early twenty first centuries. We will look at new and emerging religious realities, shifts within family traditions, and appropriate, relevant data from studies of religious practice and behavior.

As we move into Chapter Two, we will explore the implications of this changed context. We will examine the potential causes of tension and how they affect day-to-day relational life. Where children are involved, we will touch on the key operative issues in the rearing of children and, within family frameworks, how differing religious views affect the ritualization and discussion about significant life passages.

In Chapter Three, we will enter into a detailed look at the variations in religious beliefs. In an attempt to be expansive and as inclusive as possible, we will examine these variations in the broader context of exploring a working definition of religion and looking at the clear implications inherent in that definition. Chapter Four will move past this into the area of common varied religious practices and some of the emotions attached to the accommodations individuals may make in their relational situations. These chapters are intended to get into the practical details involved whenever people who are close to one another see religious matters differently.

Chapter Five explicitly contends that there are positive strengths involved in relationships which involve different religious worldviews. In this chapter, I attempt to examine these strengths thoroughly! Chapter Six builds on this by identifying specific suggestions and practical strategies for couples and families. The final chapter focuses on theological conclusions I wish to explore within the practical reality of diverse religious beliefs and practices within close human relationships and in it I argue for a solid unity within relational situations which are imbued with diversity and difference.

At the end of each chapter in this book, you will find questions for discussion and/or personal reflection. I encourage you to use these questions in ways that you find helpful. My expectation is that some of you may be reading this on your own, for personal interest, and that others may be doing so as a means to further discussion with someone you love dearly. I hope that this book will become a resource for those leading marriage preparation programs within religious institutions and that these questions may be helpful in that regard. I also encourage couples and families reading this book on their own and for their own benefit to take time to explore their responses to these questions as well. While I would really love for the questions I pose to be part of a conversation for couples speaking privately or within a shared group situation, I encourage everyone reading this book to pay careful attention to each of these questions which I have included within these pages.

This book is written with the firm conviction that how we respond to life's great questions is important. I believe that the task of religion is crucial to the human enterprise, too crucial to be ignored in the relationships that are most intimate to each of our very selves.

I hope you find our shared exploration helpful in your life!

QUESTIONS FOR DISCUSSION OR PERSONAL REFLECTION BEFORE YOU MOVE ON

1. What led you to pick up this book?
2. What do you hope to gain from reading and/or discussing it?
3. What particular issues do you hope the author explores in it?
4. In your view, what is the most difficult issue you can think of in relation to this topic?
5. What has been your life experience with the subject matter described in this introduction?
6. What do you think of the author's contention that some approaches to these religious questions could be potentially problematic in interpersonal relationships, e.g. the fundamentalist Christian who thinks the unbelieving spouse might be on the road to hell?

A CONVERSATION STARTER

For our consideration: As you begin to read this book, please consider these situations and look for opportunities to discuss them:

SOME REAL LIFE SITUATIONS

A. Megan and John see themselves as 'very much in love.' They expect to be engaged to marry very soon. They have lived together for the past six months. Megan is a Catholic and was raised in a family where Sunday church attendance was expected. Throughout her twenty six years, with rare exceptions, Megan has attended Sunday Mass. Megan and John both want to have children and Mary's preference would be to raise them in the Catholic faith, with Catholic elementary and/or high school a definite option.

John, on the other hand, was baptized in a Protestant church but his family did not attend church very often. He did not participate in Sunday School and was never confirmed. While he says he 'believes in God,' he has no interest in ever attending church and while he does not object to Mary's desire to raise children Catholic, he does not intend to participate in any church activities with them. He would prefer to spend his Sunday mornings doing housework, spending time with his children or, if he has free time, playing golf.

B. Andrew and Mary have recently gotten engaged. Andrew was raised in the Jewish faith, made his Bar Mitzvah and engages in the practice of Temple worship on occasion. Ideally, he would like a Jewish wedding ceremony and to raise future children in the Jewish tradition. Mary, raised a Protestant Christian, has fond memories of Sunday School, Christmas Pageants, Youth Group and Christian summer camp. While deeply respectful of Judaism, she is inclined to want to attend Christian services, at least on Christmas and Easter and would prefer to have her children baptized.

C. David and Lisa have been living together for nearly a year. Lisa was raised Catholic and considers herself a strong believer in God and in prayer. They love each other very much but freely admit that their religious approaches are radically different from one another. David believes quite strongly that a God does not exist, though he is willing to refer to himself as more an agnostic than a pure atheist. Lisa is bothered by this for a wide variety of reasons and David has a difficult time understanding the importance of religious faith in Lisa's life.

D. Bill and John are married to one another. Both were raised in a Christian tradition. Bill was raised Roman Catholic and has harbored strong concerns about what he perceives to be the unwillingness of the Catholic Church to condone same sex marriages. John was raised in a conservative Protestant tradition and shares some of the same concerns. They both believe in God and have faith in the person and teachings of Jesus. They would like to be part of a church, but are hesitant as well because of the experiences in their respective backgrounds.

QUESTIONS FOR THE READER

Consider and, where possible, discuss each of the following in relation to EACH of the three situations:

1. What possible future problems might occur in this relationship?
2. What can each couple do to overcome these problems?
3. What would you encourage each couple to avoid?
4. Is this relationship doomed to failure? Why? Why Not?
5. In order of difficulty, which of these situations do you find most difficult to resolve? Please explain why.

CHAPTER ONE

CHANGED RELIGIOUS REALITIES

As years move on, I believe that we Americans will realize even more deeply than we did at the time exactly how significant the 1960 Presidential election really was. When John F. Kennedy defeated Richard M. Nixon by an extremely narrow margin, the United States had elected its first Roman Catholic President. The events of the campaign that year indicated the level of controversy this electoral contest engendered.[6] Throughout both the primaries and the general election, Senator Kennedy faced major opposition from voters, including blocs of organized religious leaders, who felt that it was dangerous for the country to elect a Roman Catholic to the nation's highest office.

The fact that this election was controversial for this reason is indicative of religious realities that existed within this country at that point in its history. In the late 1950's and early 1960's, before the advent of the many sweeping social changes that bubbled to the surface in the later 1960's and beyond, one could describe the nation's religious landscape as tribal. In other words, to a great extent, Americans lived out their lives within their own religious tradition. Some critics might deride this situation as actually living in a 'religious ghetto' in which one's life was, to a great extent, governed by one's religious upbringing. This had implications for the schools individuals attended, the way they viewed other religious groups,

---

6 There has been considerable writing about this issue within several biographies of John Fitzgerald Kennedy and political reporting concerning the 1960 election. For a look at this issue in a way that examines fully the historical implications, I suggest David J. O'Brien, *The Renewal of American Catholicism* (New York: Paulist Press, 1972). A very helpful recent book that deals with the significance of the Kennedy Presidency is Chris Matthews, *JFK: Elusive Hero* (New York: Simon and Schuster, 2011).

the friends with whom they associated [7] and to a great degree, even those people whom most of them would eventually marry.

This period in time within American culture, while being an academic interest of mine, is also much more. It is the time frame in which I came of age.[8] The statistics used to describe those bygone days are reflective of my own life throughout my childhood and adolescence. I grew up in a small mill town, Putnam, Connecticut, a French Canadian Roman Catholic boy in a community that had been primarily Catholic since its inception and was heavily influenced by French Canadian culture. Many of the mills in Putnam and surrounding towns were run by owners who were Protestant. While Putnam had several active and prominent Protestant churches, the largest church of them all was St. Mary's Catholic Church, my home parish. In addition, Putnam was the national home of a religious community of nuns, the Daughters of the Holy Spirit, who staffed St. Mary's School, which I attended, as well as Putnam Catholic Academy, the all girls high school which was the *alma mater* of my mother and a great number of young women from my home town.

While there most certainly were exceptions, the fact remains that the overwhelming number of marriages in Putnam and communities similar to it were between people with the same religious background. This was hardly exclusive to Eastern Connecticut or even the Northeast for that matter. What I describe about my life is very typical of communities throughout most of the United States in the 'baby boom' years which followed the end of World War II.[9] The mothers and fathers of my peers were, for the most part,

---

7   In the nineteenth century, there was considerable growth in secondary school and collegiate institutions which held particular ethnic group/religious affiliations.

8   For a fuller, detailed description of this time period in my life in relationship to the larger questions involved, please see my book *Crossing the Street* (Gonzalez, Florida: Energion Publications, 2012).

9   'Baby boom' is the popular term referring to the large number of children born after World War Two.

Catholics who married each other or, in some cases, Catholics who married Protestants who opted to become Catholics at the time of the marriage.[10] The same allegiance to marrying within one's own tradition held true for the Protestants in town, as well as the very small number of Jewish families.

Catholic heritage was preserved and reinforced in Putnam through a very active elementary school, St. Mary's, operated by the local parish. While some Catholic children did attend the Putnam public schools, those educational institutions were seen by the Catholics in town as the 'Protestant schools,'[11] as their student body composition reflected that heritage, as well as that of the Jewish children who lived in the community.

While there are unique qualities associated with a small mill town, for sure, my experience in Putnam reflected a reality played out in ethnic communities in big cities as well. (If you want to see an excellent, accurate portrayal of these realities, you may want to check out some episodes of the popular television series *Blue Bloods* which depicts the lives of three generations of a New York Irish Catholic family.)

My wife, for example, grew up Irish Catholic in the large city of Hartford, Connecticut's capital. It was a city teeming with Catholic elementary schools which tended to service the families of varied ethnicities.[12] At the time she was growing up, the Catholic Archdiocese of Hartford made a major push to build local Catholic high schools, one of which she eventually would attend and from which she would graduate. While these cities tended to get more

---

10 In the late 1950's and early 1960's, there was high expectation that Protestants who married Catholics would choose to become Catholics themselves. In Catholic circles, this was known as a 'mixed marriage.'

11 Interestingly enough, in these schools, when prayer was allowed, the Protestant version of the Lord's Prayer was used, as were readings from the King James Bible.

12 This was typical of Catholic schools in urban areas, as they were built to serve the needs of the children of the local parish, who lived in neighborhoods where ethnicity was held in common.

Catholic students in public schools than towns such as Putnam did, they also had parishes with extremely active Catholic Youth Organizations (CYO). The CYO sponsored such events as outings, sports contests and dances where Catholic girls would just happen to meet Catholic boys! Even beyond that, the Catholic Young Adult Club was an important part of the social life of Catholic singles who were well past high school age. As a matter of fact, my wife's oldest sister met her husband through this Catholic organization. Newman clubs (a Catholic campus ministry organization) on the campuses of public universities also served the purposes of reinforcing Catholic faith and providing social opportunities for young men and women raised Catholic who were students in these secular, pluralistic environs. Large Newman Centers were quite active on secular campuses such as the University of California, Berkeley, The Ohio State University and, closer to my home, the University of Connecticut.

Throughout the course of the 1960's and the decades beyond, major societal shifts have affected all aspects of American life, including the field of religious practice. When I was growing up Catholic in the 1960's, it was typical for Catholic parents to bring their children to weekly Mass. As a matter of fact, though school was not in session on Sunday mornings, St. Mary's school children were expected to sit together at the 8:00 am Sunday Mass and attendance was taken by our teacher, one of the nuns! This is the same period of time that shows high Sunday School attendance among Protestant children.[13] An end result of individual lives affected both by shared practice and the inculcation of religious truths all within the context of tribal identity was a natural tendency of individuals to then proceed to 'marry within their own' and to begin a life raising children as they were raised.

It should be noted that the proliferation of Catholic higher educational institutions also helped in this regard. While a large number of Catholic colleges were single sex schools, there were

13 These are considered to be the 'glory days' of American church attendance!

many schools of the opposite sex which offered opportunities for social interaction for Catholic young men and women. I, for example, attended Holy Cross, a Massachusetts Catholic college. For my first two years there, we were a single sex institution. However, during that time, it was typical to have weekend dances held at our school to which large numbers of Catholic women's colleges in the area were invited. Many long term relationships emerged from these social opportunities.

The situation in 2015, at the time of the writing of this book, is quite different and has been so for several years. Statistics published in 2007 indicated that 37% of American married persons are married to someone of a different religious affiliation. Current data shows that among couples married since 2010, 39% describe themselves as in "religiously mixed" marriages. In addition, the 2007 statistics show that 28% of Americans had left the faith in which they were raised. In a growing phenomenon, 22.8% of Americans now fall into the category of the 'nones,' i.e. those without religious affiliation, up from 16% just eight years ago. There are strong indicators of movement in and out of various traditions.[14]

The lives of many American families reflect these statistics. I can speak to this from personal experience. Raised a Roman Catholic, I left the church of my youth in middle age and became a Protestant, married now for nearly thirty five years to a woman who remains Roman Catholic. Our daughter, a Catholic Ph.D. student in theology, is married to a young man who was raised Southern Baptist and has not become a Catholic. They met at the historically Protestant[15] Yale Divinity School. If one were to go further and look at my extended family, one would find a wide variety of religious affiliations and practices reflective of what has been occurring in the

---

14 See http://religions.pewforum.org/. As noted above, an updated report was released in 2015, just prior to this book's publication.

15 Interestingly enough, in recent years, the largest number of students at Yale Divinity, my Catholic daughter's *alma mater*, have been Roman Catholics, the majority of whom have been women.

15

broader culture. As a matter of fact, this is often a topic at extended family gatherings.[16]

These anecdotal situations from our own family are indicative of larger realities:

- While religious preference does remain a factor in establishing interpersonal relationships and commitments, it no longer holds the influence it once did. While certain groups, e.g. Hindus (90%), Mormons (83%) and others, continue to tend to form long term relationships, there is much more fluidity in this regard among most other religious groups.

- These changes pose issues for couples regarding the specifics of their own relationships as well as in situations where children are involved.

- These situations often include tensions between generations in families of these individuals. Many couples find resistance from parents, grandparents or siblings and this resistance often flares up around times of shared family rituals. Coming out of a Christian context as I do, I can speak here of the power of the Baptism ritual and the impact it has on families in which a parent is raised as a Christian. I have seen the possibility of a baptism potentially not occurring as a major cause of anguish within Christian families.

- Couples have to face a variety of decisions that affect their own individual religious faith and practice. As examples, individuals must determine whether they plan to retain religious practices from their own tradition or seek to find common ground with their partner or spouse.

- In some cultural contexts, couples face the concern that intermarriage might lead to the negative effect of a significant loss of a culture or heritage. In thinking about this, I cannot help

---

16 My wife's parents were both Irish Catholics. Her father immigrated to this country from Ireland. A wide variety of religious affiliations exist among their grandchildren and other relatives, myself included.

remembering a situation which led to significant insights for me at a relatively young age.

Early in my college career, I became friends with a young man who, at that point, was one of two Jewish students at my Catholic college. Interestingly enough, the other Jewish student at my college, Holy Cross, went on to an outstanding career as a rabbi. My friend's father also happened to be a distinguished rabbi. My friend invited me to spend a weekend at his home and to share with the family in Sabbath dinner and then worship at the Temple, the place of worship for their Reform Jewish congregation.

As we were seated at table enjoying a delicious meal and good conversation, I asked the rabbi what I thought was a pretty basic question: 'Rabbi, what is your sermon going to be about this evening?'

He responded to me rather quickly: 'Well, Bob, I am preaching about intermarriage between Jews and Christians.'

I came back with a quick and honest response: 'Rabbi, I think that is great! You know, there is too much prejudice between Jews and Christians. We've got to get beyond that and accept intermarriage!'

His response to me was even quicker and was accompanied by a stern, serious look: 'Bob, I am preaching **against** it!'

At that point, I felt like hiding under the table. Instead I took refuge in some delicious chicken soup!

Through this uncomfortable, but honest, interaction, I learned something very important about the complexity of some of these questions. While my comment reflected what I thought was a healthy sense of religious openness born of my evolving 1960's affected liberalism, the rabbi's response led me to realize that these issues are really multi layered. To a community which was virtually wiped out in the horrors of the Holocaust not even thirty years prior to this conversation, it is understandable how intermarriage could be a threat that evoked the fears attached to the possible annihilation of one's culture and way of being.

Over the course of time, the Jewish community has dealt with this issue in a variety of ways as considerable interrelating and intermarrying has occurred. As I point out later in this chapter, some significant writing has been done on this topic and much magnificent reflection on lived experience. This movement reflects the trend which has been existent in society for years and is far different from the context in which I was raised.

This trend involving significant shifts within traditions has many implications. Among them, as we have noted here, is the fear many have of the possible extinction or radical diminishing of the tradition itself. Over the years, as I reflected more deeply upon the horrors of the Holocaust, I grew in my appreciation of this serious concern. Within that broader context lies the very human reality that couples meet and fall in love and as a result of that love may choose to have children. Dealing with these conflicting realities can cause consternation and anguish.

On the other hand, there are strong indications that many couples and families are moving in the direction of a different approach. Susan Katz Miller has written a recent book entitled *Being Both: Embracing Two Religions in One Interfaith Family*[17] which explores this issue with an entirely different perspective. In it, she advocates for the viability of truly interfaith couples and families! I encourage readers to get your hands on a copy of Ms. Katz Miller's book and discuss it carefully. In many ways, it is a ground breaking work and deeply thought provoking! She poses questions, in my view, which cause one to look at the universal wisdom to be found in diverse religious experiences and expression.

Less significant, in my view, yet also quite real, is the fear among many religious people that intermarriage and other long term relational commitments are indicators that one's particular

---

17 See Susan Katz Miller, *Being Both: Embracing Two Religions in One Interfaith Family* (Boston: Beacon Press, 2013).

faith tradition is in the process of losing what it once had. Examining the Christian tradition, for example, in the lifetime of baby boomers such as I, Catholics, Protestant and Orthodox Christians alike have experienced the closing of many of their churches and other related church institutions,[18] declining attendance and an aging process within their congregations which has led many to fear the impending demise of the Christian church within this culture.[19] While this is a topic within many religious institutions, and many leaders have advocated that congregations think of things differently from how they have in the past, the prospect of possible closure of cherished religious buildings is quite painful for many to take.

It is within this broad context that, as has been the case for time eternal, individuals meet, fall in love and strongly consider committing themselves to one another for life! My hope and conviction is that couples from different religious backgrounds and perspectives can engage in serious discussion about their backgrounds as it relates to both their shared present and future. I hope that they can do this without feeling that they must avoid their own religious journey in the process. In fact, I would go so far as to argue instead that, within the framework of the love they share, through the process of dialogue with their beloved, their own journey may be enhanced considerably, even if different from the journey lived by the one whom they love the most!

---

18 Church mergers and closings have been a great concern among these groups. In one of my books (*Part Time Pastor, Full Time Church* (Cleveland: The Pilgrim Press, 2010), I explore the impact of these changing realities on the way leadership functions in the contemporary church.

19 This possibility has been explored in much of the conversation that has occurred within church contexts.

QUESTIONS FOR DISCUSSION AND CONSIDERATION

1. Consider talking to a parent or grandparent and asking her/ him about how she/he perceive the differences in religious practice between now and when that person was your age.

2. In what ways can religious differences affect a relationship between two people?

3. What do you see as good specific strategies for couples in dealing with their own religious differences?

4. What strategies would you see as detrimental to dealing with religious differences in relationships?

5. What do you think about this statement: 'A couple in love should not argue about religion'?

CHAPTER TWO

WHAT ARE THE ISSUES?

When couples are so serious in their relationships that they decide to make a long term commitment to one another, they must confront a variety of issues, all of which have serious implications, including the potential to rupture the relationship despite any strong emotional bond that may exist. Couples need to take a good close look at how they approach financial matters, the ways their work time and their time together balance, their individual professional aspirations, how they deal with each other's family of origin and a variety of other important issues.

High on the list of topics and situations which must be confronted are those involving religious belief and practice. While these matters may intensify once children enter the scene, if they do, they might very well flare up to an uncomfortable level prior to their birth or adoption. Even in the absence of potential or very real offspring, these issues may drive a wedge between those who will claim most assuredly that they are very much in love. There are many reasons for this. While what we will discuss in this chapter is not an all inclusive compendium of potential danger, we will be looking here at some key issues which could be particularly problematic. As you think about and discuss what you are reading in this book, perhaps you will consider even more. For now, here's a start at looking at these potential pitfalls. As you read through these, you may want to go back and look at the conversation starters I included at the beginning of this book, as well as those you will find throughout these chapters.[20]

---

20 Here is a reminder to be sure to explore these conversation starters!

As a way of entering this process, I suggest we look at several plausible, real life complications involving couples and their own families of origin. We will do this by exploring this one situation.

> **Example:** One of the individuals really wants to practice her/his faith and would like the other to share in what that faith means. At the same time, the other individual, for whatever reason, is just not interested.

I imagine that as you consider what I have written, you can identify further examples from your own experience. As you identify them, please think about discussing them with the one(s) which whom you may be sharing this book. Here are some potential problems:

1. As a result of this difference, a difference really about **religion**, there is a tension within the couple's relationship. As I see it, this is not to say that a relationship cannot be good should shared faith be absent. It is to point out that the absence of a religious perspective held in common can leave one partner with the feeling that she/he is not sharing something so intimately close that it is integral in articulating the meaning of the relationship itself. In an obvious example, we might consider the man who sees his love for his spouse as being blessed by or willed by God. Should his spouse see this kind of thinking as non reflective of her/his own, this man may feel some kind of emotional void. This is not to say that, in and of itself, a difference of opinion indicates a problem in the relationship. To the contrary, many successful marriages exist between atheists and believers.. In fact, and this is equally important, it is very easy to hold to a surface level, unexamined perspective on what it means for God to bless or will a relationship and, in the religious realm, there are different ways in which people understand those statements theologically. In my view, all too often spiritual language lives within the realm of the unexamined cliche. This can be harmful in terms of real spiritual awareness and maturity. Think

of the way "it is God's will" has been bandied around in religious conversation!

From a religious standpoint, the relationship of grace, God's will and the use of individual freedom is very complicated and the interpretations attached quite diverse. We really all need to realize that no simple statement spoken aloud can fully describe the nuances attached to any of our religious convictions. In fact, the presence of faith in God in one's life involves the profound recognition that one cannot fully express the heart and essence of God.[21]

Nonetheless, someone deeply committed to another and madly in love may feel a pang of regret that her/his beloved does not share a common belief or practice. While distinctions exist between 'mixed' belief and 'mixed' practice, there are potentially problematic emotional reactions attached to each.

2. The potential exists for exacerbated tension among extended families. Parents and siblings deeply invested in the religious perspective of one member of the couple may make life uncomfortable for that individual and/or her/his partner. Religion can become a battleground in the extended relationship context. If one considers the emotional investment some parents have made in raising their children Catholic or Jewish, to use but two of many examples, one can see the potential for complicated emotional reactions in this regard. This can really flare up when it is time to celebrate holidays where families usually come together.

The other side of the coin is that holidays which were once celebrated with the 'religious meaning' at core now take on a different significance. They become gatherings that focus on the family as the central, core belief. Children and grandchildren who have not attended Christmas services show up at the family dinner table to celebrate Christmas. It is fair to say that in many families, this lack

---

21 I think, for example, of Soren Kierkegaard's notion that, to a significant extent, faith always requires a 'leap.' In the words of Hebrews 11, it supplies "the evidence of things not seen."

of connection to the religious significance of this shared holiday is bothering someone!!

3. Following up on the previous point, the perspective of those connected to the couple in an extended situation may spill over into issues involving the religious education and practice of children. There may be similarities in how this plays out even when there are specific peculiarities unique to particular religious traditions. For example, a devout Catholic family might very well envision the First Communion ritual as an important rite of passage and extended family celebration. Problems might arise when the couple opts not to put a daughter/son through a First Communion program. There are multiple layers to the emotions attached to this and it is here where the effects of the changes in religious practice within our society really tend to hit some individuals very hard.

In addition, as noted above, there may be certain family events centered on religious practice that take on a different look because of a family member's relationship. Shared rituals such as family funerals, weddings, feast days such as Christmas or Hanukkah, etc. may be the cause of adjustment and turmoil.

As we will say in several places and in different ways, an important key to handling this situation is for the couple to engage in honest conversation **as early as possible**. Simply put, this is not something that should be swept under the rug in a relationship. Oftentimes, people are tempted to do so in an effort to 'keep the peace', only to regret it because the issues involved eventually come back to take center stage.

As we proceed in this book, we will examine this even more closely. In writing this, I recognize that I cannot account for all specific situations. What I am hoping is that I am able to get you thinking in universal terms, i.e. the impact of religious differences and practices upon each individual within the relationship and, when children may be involved, the potential impact upon them. Yet, for now, we need to move in another direction, albeit closely related. We need to explore the potential variations in religious expressions that could exist between partners. We do so as a way of recognizing not only the complexity of the questions we are exploring but also of the unique bond that is each loving relationship!

QUESTIONS FOR DISCUSSION

1. Have you known couples who, in your view, have 'successfully navigated' their religious differences? What do you know and think about how they did it?

2. To what extent, in your view, can different religious points of view be harmful to a relationship?

3. What might work for a couple which has to deal with religious tension coming from extended family members?

4. Have you experienced this change in focus of family celebrations such as Christmas or Passover, for example? What do you think of the author's comments about the Christmas celebration where family members have not attended services?

5. In *Being Both*, Susan Katz Miller makes a powerful argument in favor of families living as "interfaith families," i.e. truly sharing in the living out of more than one religious tradition. What do you think? Doable? Problematic?

CHAPTER THREE

THE VARIETIES OF
RELIGIOUS EXPRESSION

In order to address the importance of communication between partners on matters of religion, we need to make an honest exploration regarding the reality of religion's complexity. It is not enough to discuss the differences between Catholics and Protestants or Jews and Christians as they apply to interpersonal relations and the potential rearing of children. In fact, we all know fully well that different ways of thinking and practicing the faith exist between those who 'share the same religion,' e.g. not all Catholics (or other religious groupings, for that matter) interpret their faith approach in the same way. The reality is that there is great religious diversity within the traditions themselves. Instead it seems preferable to place the questions and issues which arise within a broader context, that of the wide expanse of religious understanding itself.

Religious expression comes in a multiplicity of forms. This reality begs an exploration into the very nature of religion. Therefore, we need to raise this question: In the broadest and purest sense, what do we mean when we use the word religion? In other words, before we look at the obstacles, impediments and strengths involved in 'interreligious' relationships, we need to explore the dynamics involved in the development of one's personal religious approach.

To this end, I would like to introduce a simple (and I think inclusive) definition of religion. What I am saying is that it is not enough to define religion in terms of belonging to an organized self identified religious group. This broader definition I propose is drawn from my personal integration of a wide variety of readings in the field of religious studies over a rather long period of time.[22]

---

22 Actually, I credit the work of Ronald Wilkins, a Catholic religious educator, for his popularization of this approach. I was able to use his framework in

In simple terms, my preference is to define religion as *one's personal approach to the mystery of life.*

By this short, direct definition, what I am suggesting is that each of us human beings go through life with a need to deal with its mysteries. In other words, there is an awful lot we don't know. When we are thrust into this world, we are concurrently thrust into a sea of mystery. We seek answers to profound questions within us, even if we don't think of ourselves as overly philosophical. The ways in which we grapple with life's questions are reflected in our literary and cinematic expressions, as well as in the world of the music to which we listen.[23] Even further, I would look to break down these areas of mystery into three important groupings. I would suggest that we all have to come to terms with how we respond to life's mysteries of *origin, destiny* and *meaning.* Thus, this way of examining the issue of religion is centered on the fact that there are distinct ways of *APPROACHING* certain complex universal human questions. It presupposes that these key human questions are, in fact, *religious* questions i.e. they deal with life's ultimate concerns, *universal* to all human beings, regardless of 'religious affiliation.'

In presenting this perspective to varied religious groups over the years, it has become clear to me that presenting these issues as 'mysterious' in some way runs counter to the understanding many of us have that our religious perspective offers answers that are absolute and certain. In some traditions, the source for the absolute answer is Scripture. In others, the authority of the religious body, e.g., the church.

By mysteries of origin, I would suggest that we all go through life without **really** knowing how life itself really began. **We were not there** and so we naturally proceed to theorize about what really

teaching comparative religion in Roman Catholic high schools in the 1980's. His textbook *The Religions of Man* (Dubuque: William C. Brown, 1967) was very helpful.

23 In my years as a teacher of religion, I spent considerable classroom time with students exploring the messages in contemporary music that explore these ultimate questions. I found this process helpful for them.

happened. We choose sources to either accept or reject, based on what we have been taught or what we have experienced. The tension between what we have learned through experience and what we have been taught as ways of explaining mystery can be a great source of religious tension.

Some of us might attribute authority on life's mysteries to a particular book which we have deemed to be sacred. Others opt for as scientific an understanding as we construct. How we look upon the different sources for our religious understanding is a fundamental dividing line between and among religious perspectives. Whether we share a literal, creationist perspective, are supporters of 'intelligent design' or adhere to a theory of evolution,[24] we all share in the simple reality that when it all began, we were not there. Thus, we are left to speculate, theorize, or take some kind of leap of faith.

The same fact applies to *mysteries of destiny*. By this, we are referring to those questions about the future- our personal futures as well as that of this planet and universe which we currently inhabit. Individuals choose up sides: Is there a heaven? A hell? A purgatory? If there is, what is it like? Literature and music are peppered with all kinds of variations: different descriptions of heaven, theories about hell and so on.[25] Some authors and composers speak with absolute certainty of their **exact** knowledge about all the mysteries of life after death. Most of us speak in terms of a faith, albeit many 'believers', myself included, prefer to speak of a reasonable faith. By this I mean a faith that is not contradicted by human reason.[26] Yet, even among those of us who do posit belief in those terms, there lies a recognition that for faith to be faith, it requires a certain leap into the unknown, that which Luther referred to as *fiducia*, an

---

24 The theory associated with the work of Charles Darwin.

25 Works such as *Dante's Inferno* are well known in this regard and a serious look at the plays of Shakespeare, for example, shows great preoccupation with these themes. Some interpretations of Shakespeare's *Hamlet* have placed great emphasis upon these issues as explored in this classic work.

26 This is in, though not limited to, the tradition of scholastic philosophy closely associated with Thomas Aquinas.

approach which moves the believer beyond intellectual affirmation into the realm of trust in the reality that is God.[27] Likewise, linked with the matter of the afterlife, we recognize that the when and how and if of whether the world as we know it will end is a topic laden with variety and substantial controversy.[28]

In teaching this concept to people, I like to cite two very well known, fairly contemporary musical sources. One is the song Imagine, written and performed by John Lennon. This song begins with these words:

> *Imagine there's no heaven,*
> *It's easy if you try.*
> *No hell below us.*
> *Above us only sky.*
> *Imagine all the people,*
> *living for today ...*

As the song goes on, the sentiment deepens:

> *Imagine there's no countries,*
> *it isn't hard to do.*
> *Nothing to kill or die for—*
> *and no religion too ...* [29]

The implication of these words is that if you take the question of eternal destiny off the table, you can focus on building a better world right here and right now. Conversely, by keeping it on the table and placing your focus on the attainment of eternal happiness, you end up neglecting what you should be concentrating on in the quite limited time you have here on this planet.

---

27 As noted above in reference to Soren Kierkegaard.

28 A plethora of works and theories have made their way on to the scene in recent years, including such writing on 'the rapture' as found in the popular *Left Behind* series.

29 John Lennon, *Imagine*.

In the 1970's, the singer/songwriter Billy Joel made this contribution to the discussion about how the way we see destiny affects the way we perceive daily life:

Oh, they say there's a heaven for those who wait.
Some say it's better but I say it ain't.
I'd rather laugh with the sinners
than cry with the saints.
The sinners are much more fun
— and only the good die young.[30]

These phrases from the world of popular music are deeply laden with implications for how individuals see the interplay of one's approach to questions of destiny and meaning in this present life. In Joel's quotation, the underlying assumption is that enjoyment in life will be found by those who are not focusing on the afterlife, in this case, not even really concerned about the eternal reward of a life well lived. These questions of destiny and meaning are deeply interconnected of course, because somewhere between where we came from, individually or collectively, and where we are going lies this present life. Consequently, we all have to make decisions regarding what constitutes life's *meaning*. In other words, we have to decide upon the values that really make life worthwhile. Many would agree that **love** is right up there as one of those values, yet we know through a cursory study of the history of our world that this popular word itself has many definitions and its value faces strong competition. It calls to mind another song, doesn't it?

Some say love –it is a river that drowns the tender reed
Some say love-it is a razor that leaves your soul to bleed
Some say love -it is a hunger, an endless aching need
I say love-it is a flower and you, its only seed.[31]

30 Billy Joel, *Only the Good Die Young.*
31 Amanda McBroom, *The Rose.*

In this beloved work, popularized by Bette Midler, the reality that love has many definitions is stated quite directly. The notion of love as a flower with the one loving providing what it needs to blossom is the preferred position of the songwriter. The very articulation of these words, in keeping with a beautiful, complementary melody, causes the listener to engage in this reflection upon that which constitutes meaning in these, our earthly lives.

In exploring these issues more deeply, it strikes me that we can conclude how human beings respond to these mysteries by taking one of three fundamental approaches:

1. They identify themselves as *believers* in the existence of the divine. In other words, many individuals would contend that there is a reality that exists beyond the discernible world of human beings, other animals and all that comprises 'the natural world.' Some would call this reality 'God.' Others might choose different words.

2. They describe themselves as *atheists*. An individual choosing this approach would rule out the presence of the divine as part of human existence. She/he would thus rule out the possibility of a life beyond this, the material world.

3. They are comfortable calling themselves *agnostics*. An agnostic, while not closed to the possibility of the divine and the spiritual, would maintain a strong conviction that she/he does not have the evidence she/he needs to identify as a believer.

What is clear in this breakdown and analysis of the varieties of religious approaches is that, lying even deeper beneath the surface of whether one is, for example, Catholic or Lutheran, is an overall approach to religion which has all kinds of implications. One, as an example, might be that conceivably, you could have a couple, both of whom are Catholic, who tend to conceptualize God in different ways.

One might find comfort in an almost literal picture of a fatherly God ruling the universe. The other might see God as more an ineffable spirit or be more attuned to an expansive language which incorporates feminine imagery.[32] One could go on and on about the really wide range of religious approaches even among those who 'share the same religion.'

Parenthetically, I am often struck when I am presiding at worship as a clergyperson that in the pews around me, there exists a wide variety of interpretations of life's greatest mysteries, even as we are speaking or singing the very same words of faith. The individuality of each person's religious approach is quite profound! What I find most intriguing, from recent published data, is the number of people who appear to be quite uninterested in the kinds of reflections that are part of what constitutes religious expression. The Pew Research report to which I have alluded, refers to an increase in the number of religiously disinterested. Despite this, I nonetheless contend that in each of our minds, we wonder about those things that really are so mysterious — *Where did we come from? Where are we going? While we are here, what's it all about?*

Now, in this regard, I would argue strongly that it is a good thing for couples to talk to each other about these matters. I would also contend though some would disagree with me, that strong religious differences, as I have defined the concept, can exist within relationships that are good, positive and loving. In other words, I would reject the notion that one has to be of the 'same religion' to have a good relationship. I fully acknowledge that there are those, within some religious traditions, who would have a serious problem with these comments of mine.

I would also, as I have said, find lacking the position that where differences exist, they should just be kept isolated and never discussed. It makes logical sense that two people may very well be raised in the same religious tradition yet, as a result of their life experiences and their own spiritual and intellectual inquiry, would differ on issues related to the nature of God, the afterlife and how

---

32 In my view, the expansion of descriptive language about God is important on many levels and should be encouraged in liturgical language and in hymns.

to apply one's faith to specific everyday moral/ethical questions. Just because two people might share a common identification, e.g. Catholic, Protestant, Jew, Muslim, does **not** mean that they should be expected to think identically on many legitimate religious issues that confront all human beings as they deal with the ultimate questions in life, those issues of our origin, our destiny and the very meaning of this everyday experience we simply call life! Evidence indicates that people within the same religious affiliation share a variety of positions on many social and political issues and how they would apply their theology and religious faith to concrete, real life ethical situations. Yet, despite these commonalities, very real differences can most assuredly still exist!

DISCUSSION QUESTIONS

1. What is your opinion of the author's use of the term 'religious approaches'?
2. Do you agree that, even when one shares the same religious approach as another, you might still have significant differences? Can you think of concrete examples you know of where this has taken place?

AN IMPORTANT INTERLUDE BEFORE WE MOVE ON

Discussion Questions for Couples and for People Facilitating Conversations between Couples

Here is a list of 'religious questions' that I would find to be of value for couples who are either serious about building a life together, raising children, or both. I don't necessarily suggest that they all be discussed in one sitting or short period of time. I **do** suggest that they become part of one's life.

A: Some questions to be sure to discuss as people are getting serious about sharing a life together:

1. Where is 'religion' in your life?
2. What term would you use to describe yourself religiously? (Examples would include but not be limited to: Christian, Jew, agnostic, seeker, spiritual, spiritual but not religious ...)
3. What have been the influences in your life regarding how you view religion?
4. What's your notion of God? Describe how you envision God.
5. Do you see worship as part of your future life? If marrying: Do you want to be married in a 'religious' ceremony? Why or why not? In a house of worship?
6. (For those who are open to having children:) What is your view of raising children religiously?
7. (Where there is significant difference in religious approach or religious affiliation:) What are we going to decide upon in terms of raising children?
8. Will we pray at home? At meals? With children if we have them? What prayer style will we use?
9. (Where one individual wishes to worship and the other does not:) Will you ever attend worship with me? Will you come to non-worship events at my place of worship? Will you attend children's activities at my place of worship even if you do not attend?
10. (Underlying all of this if significant differences exist:) How will we resolve our differences in a way that allows us to be faithful to what we believe? Is there anything that is really a non negotiable. An example of this would be: 'I am always going to want to attend Midnight Mass at Christmas' or 'I insist that if we have children, they are going to be baptized.'

B: Some deeper questions, as a relationship evolves, I think these questions are important:

1. GOD

a.   What is your image? What do you think of when you think of God?

b.   How important is prayer? Do you pray? How do you think it works? How do you think God handles prayer?

c.   If a Christian, what is your understanding of Jesus?

2. Religious Practices

a.   What belief/practices of your partner is/are most difficult for you to understand?

b.   What is your personal approach concerning the celebration of holidays that have religious significance?

c.   Is God active in our lives? How?

d.   How do you think God views your relationship? Does God 'view' things? Does God see all?

e.   Do you believe God has a plan for all of us? What does this mean?

C: A personal opinion from the author:

Please consider this and discuss it. I am writing this in the first person because it is my opinion. I am convinced, based on my experience of working with engaged couples, that most really don't pay enough attention to the nitty gritty of building a successful marriage. This includes, but is not limited to, the discussion of these important questions of 'religion.'

Honestly, what I have seen is that, during the engagement period, for example, there is so much emphasis on the glitz and glitter of the wedding 'event' that the most important aspect gets lost- what it takes to build a life together. Before anyone makes a commitment to another, they have to face the important questions.

What I am saying is that if you have not faced some of this stuff, it could get really ugly when you can't agree on having your baby baptized or whether you are going to sign her up for Sunday School. It is better to face the really tough questions as early as possible!

CHAPTER 4

COMMON RELIGIOUS VARIATIONS IN COUPLES

While there are variations in approaches that transcend particular allegiances to religious traditions, it is important to explore some typical, popularly identifiable, differences that exist between couples. In looking at the United States, with its history and tradition of religious pluralism and diversity, we can catch a good glimpse of some of the most noteworthy among these differences. Below you will find the common varieties of interreligious relationships. While the listing does not account for them all, it is intended to provide a helpful overview.

1. Relationships between a Catholic and a Protestant
2. Relationships between a Christian and a Jew
3. Relationships between a believer and an agnostic or atheist
4. Relationships between one who a 'practicing' member of a faith tradition and someone who does not 'practice,' oftentimes including a couple, both of whom have the same religious background
5. Relationships between practicing Christians and Jews and those of Islamic, Buddhist or Hindu traditions

It is important that we begin by examining the unique components involved in each of these possible relationships:

RELATIONSHIPS BETWEEN A CATHOLIC AND A PROTESTANT

Throughout the history of the United States, this has been the predominant example of interreligious relationships. It is also the relationship with which I am most familiar as I happen to be a Protestant married to a Roman Catholic woman. My situation in this regard is a tad unique, however, as for the first eighteen years of our marriage, my wife and I were both practicing Catholics. My wife's presumption at the time of our marriage was that I would be a lifelong Catholic.

The key issues that arise within these relationships come to the surface when each member of the couple chooses to continue the active practice of her/his faith or when questions involving the religious education of children enter the picture. In some cases, the Catholic Church's position on a particular moral question could have an impact upon the relationship. As an example, I would cite a relationship in which one of the partners believes he/she has the obligation to comply with the church's teaching on contraception and the other does not. Given the widespread practice of contraception among Catholics, this tends not to be the divisive issue it would have been in 1960,[33] Nonetheless, it could pose problems in some relationships.

In practical terms, individuals may find themselves at religious services and activities while their partners are at different worship services of their own or may opt not to worship at all. Current data indicates that this is often likely to occur in this manner: The women are at church while the men are at home, on the golf course or at Home Depot. The absence of men in organized religious settings is a concern that churches have addressed in recent years in a variety of ways.

RELATIONSHIPS BETWEEN A CHRISTIAN AND A JEW

In this situation, members of each tradition who tend to adhere to its practices must determine if they will continue to do so

---

33 As the 1960's unfolded, a chasm was developing in the Catholic Church between those who favored the traditional teaching and those couples who opted to use birth control. Division existed in the church between the hierarchy and theologians who believed the teaching should be upheld and others who favored significant reform. While adherents to the traditional teaching do remain in the Catholic Church, the practice of using artificial contraception is common among Catholic couples. While official Catholic teaching remains opposed to artificial means of contraception, Catholic practice has moved decisively in a different direction.

or will seek to select one tradition over the other as the religious practice of the couple or family. When children are part of the relationship, decisions must be reached regarding their education and how holidays are celebrated as part of home life. There is a growing movement of those who are open to relationships in which individuals celebrate both religious traditions and overtly seek expressions of interconnection. I encourage the reader to delve deeply into the writings of Susan Katz Miller, previously cited.

RELATIONSHIPS BETWEEN BELIEVERS AND AGNOSTICS OR ATHEISTS

In many cases, even non practicing believers may have an interest in some degree of participation in religious practice, usually those centered around holidays or involving children. How a nonbeliever responds to that can be a cause for tension. Defining "believer" broadly would include accepting as believers those who would define themselves as "spiritual but not religious."

RELATIONSHIPS BETWEEN PRACTITIONERS AND NONPRACTITIONERS

Potential for tension can arise within couples where there is a difference in practice. Individuals may begin to feel that they are not sharing a vital, integral part of their life with their partners. If/when children come, this difference can be even more exacerbated.

RELATIONSHIPS BETWEEN CHRISTIANS AND JEWS AND THOSE OF ISLAMIC, HINDU AND BUDDHIST TRADITIONS

While there has been a sad, pathetic history of anti-Semitism within our culture and our world, there is a unique compatibility between Jews and Christians which is often under-appreciated. There are deep commonalities that can help form a natural bond and a basis for shared life, including when children are involved. Since Christians and Jews often have less familiarity with Eastern religions and with Islam, there is a lot of religious information they need to learn, information to which they may not have been previously exposed.

Also worth commenting upon is the dynamic involved when an individual within the relationship changes religious course at some point in the couple's life together. While we are focusing on discussing as many of these issues as possible beforehand, reality makes clear that these changes occur at various times. Such is the case in my own marriage. As I see it, the key, as in all of these situations, lies in an honest sharing of what is going on inside of oneself. I am most confident in saying that when I decided to contemplate leaving Catholicism, my wife was not surprised by the thought process that led to that decision. Certainly, one can struggle with a tradition and opt not to leave it and thus the moment of decision almost inevitably comes as some surprise. This is not as problematic, however, as what is perceived as some sudden, previously hidden, shift in belief! Having said this, we must also assert that if it MOVES one to a tradition which views the other simply as wrong, this can become a source of significant tension and distress.

Regardless of the particularity of the relationship, there are also some typical ways in which couples have approached how they handle these differences. These tend to be the most common:

1. A couple is at peace with the fact that each will adhere to an approach different from the other. In the case of the individual who believes that his/her understanding is the "truth" and the other approach is false, how much can one really be at peace is a good question, isn't it? One has to at least posit the POSSIBILITY that certain religious shifts could cause irreparable harm to a relationship. (HINT: Maybe you can discuss this!)

2. One of the two moves outside of her/his upbringing or preference and participates to whatever degree s/he is comfortable.

3. When children are involved, they opt to raise them 'neutrally' or when belief is involved, within both traditions, again to whatever extent is possible.

4. When children are involved, one member of the couple accepts the child being raised in the tradition of the other member.

5. Couples seek a 'neutral' solution wherein they agree on a religious approach that meets them halfway. In Christian-interfaith relations, Unitarianism is a tradition that oftentimes serves as a 'bridge' tradition for couples and families. I have seen this happen in congregations of the United Church of Christ as well as in other local churches aligned with the 'progressive Christianity' movement.[34]

6. Individuals seek to live out a real 'interfaith' relationship/family.

An important concern in these situations has to do with the impact of these differences on the relational life of the couple. The greatest impact, as I see it, is when one member of this relationship feels unable to express her/his particular religious perspective in a satisfying way. This could happen when one feels she/he can not worship as she/he wants or conversely is somehow coerced into engaging in religious practice that makes her/him uncomfortable. This, of course, is tied into larger questions involving the importance of egalitarian relationships. This has been a challenge for many heterosexual couples wherein remnants of sexism remain. I would also add that in many conservative Christian churches, interpretations of Biblical passages concerning women and the relationship between men and women pose unique problems in this regard.[35]

---

34 These traditions hold to a 'non creedal' approach which affirms freedom of conscience and flexibility in belief/practice. In the case of Unitarianism, while one can be a Unitarian Christian, one need not affirm Jesus as Savior to be part of the Unitarian Universalist tradition.

35 Sadly, those groups who favor a Biblical interpretation that positions the husband as head of the household are, in my view, harmful in terms of making

In some Christian traditions, the notion of the male as "head of the household" mitigates against any acceptance of the possibility that the woman may legitimately seek out or practice a different approach to one's religion.

Of course, one could also contend that a fundamentalist Christian woman would have great difficulty accepting the convictions of a spouse/partner of a significantly different religious persuasion. Having said this, the relational imbalance espoused in certain interpretations of scripture renders difficult the potential for healthy "interreligious" relationships in many situations.

The bottom line is that what I am saying presupposes a significant degree of openness to a spirituality that can be found and expressed in a variety of ways. In practical terms, for example, it recognizes that a "practicing Christian" can have a healthy, even long-term relationship with a Jew, Muslim, Atheist, Agnostic, or someone else who might happen to hold to a different religious perspective.

Theologically, I see this as possible because of the operative power of LOVE which I am pleased to affirm comes from a God who is greater than all understandings we mortals of that which constitutes the divine.

As we move into the next two chapters, we will explore both the strengths inherent in these interreligious relationships as well as some suggestions and strategies that can be helpful in building on those strengths.

DISCUSSION QUESTIONS:

1. Evaluate the strengths and weaknesses of each of the five ways in which couples have handled these differences. If you are a

---

this possible. A well known group within the tradition is Promise Keepers. Also, Iron Sharpens Iron. Their tendency to interpret certain passages of Scripture in a way that favors male domination in relationships is, in my view, harmful to women and the family.

couple and something in this section applies to you, talk about your view regarding how to handle it.

2. Do you agree with the author that certain Biblical interpretations may be problematic in male-female relationships? Discuss/ Explain

3. What are some of the unique challenges facing couples wherein one partner decides to change her/his approach to religion at some point over the course of the relationship? Does the nature of the new religious approach make a difference?

4. What of yourselves do you see in these situations the author has described here?

Chapter 5
Strengths in Interreligious Relationships

I t would be easy to say that by simply devoting a lengthy piece of writing to the issues addressed in this book, the inherent assumption of the writer (and perhaps the reader) is that interreligious relationships may very well pose problems for couples. While we have pointed out the areas in which, in fact, they may, the reality is that such relationships have the potential to be extremely positive both for each individual and for the couple itself. In addition, where there are children involved, the potential for the parents' relationship to be beneficial to them is considerable as well.

As I see it, there are two fundamental reasons why such is the case:

1. Any individual involved in an interreligious relationship is in a position to develop a deepened relationship about traditions other than her/his own and in so doing, will have the opportunity to understand one's own more profoundly. Children in such relationships will be exposed to both traditions and to discussions about the relative claims of each. Let us say, hypothetically, that a devout Muslim woman is married to a Catholic man. First of all, opportunities abound to share with one another all kinds of information about the background and traditions of each faith. This occurs at a level where intense personal interest is present. Sadly, as Stephen Prothero has pointed out so clearly and accurately, there exists a certain religious illiteracy in our culture in which people simply don't know enough about the specifics of different

47

religious perspectives.[36] This personal interest might spark deeper understanding.

Even more deeply, discussions can develop within the home over profound questions of life, death and meaning. It would be natural for such a couple to explore how each other sees Jesus in relation to her/his faith. In the case of the Muslim believer, the prophet Mohammed has a unique, special significance in relation to Jesus. Examining the points of religious connection and disconnection could be most fascinating and, might I also say, wonderfully enriching.

In an increasingly diverse, pluralistic world, young people can benefit from having in depth experiential knowledge of traditions which are often misunderstood outside of the boundaries of believers who live them. Among children and adults alike, prayer life can be enriched as the Catholic may learn of Muslim practices that can enhance and enrich one's spirituality and vice versa. Perhaps there is something in the way one speaks about or worships God that can be incorporated into the spiritual life of the other and in the children of that union as well.

2. By engaging in a religious approach outside of one's own preference or upbringing, one is in a position to learn much about the thinking and practice of another tradition. The process of learning here may very well involve intense discussion and maybe even study inside of the home. This can be a very good thing! People of all ages might find themselves reading books, articles or accessing web sites about religion that would not have been part of their experience otherwise. This could go a long way toward assisting young people in gaining a healthy sense of differences that occur among people and from which they can learn more about themselves.

---

36 See the excellent development of this thought in Stephen Prothero, *Religious Literacy* (San Francisco: Harper San Francisco, 2007).

Saying this is **not** to suggest that interreligious relationships are preferable to those in which both individuals are of the same persuasion. Nor is it to say that if one is raised in a home in which parents are united in faith and practice, one is disadvantaged religiously. *In fact, my view instead is that those in homes united by religious approach need to both explore their own tradition more deeply **and** learn about other views as a means toward enhancing their understanding of their own religious affiliation.* This is a point I make in several of my other writings.[37] What I **am** saying is that in interreligious relationships, there is great potential for broadening one's own theology and sense of practice.

Consider, for example, my own home. Through the experience of being raised by a Protestant and a Catholic who are married to each other, our own three children have been in the position where they have asked a lot of questions about the commonalities and differences between Catholicism and, in our case, mainline Protestantism. By experiencing worship in Roman Catholic and Protestant churches, they have experienced worship styles and participated in discussions about the reasons behind those differences that they might never have done had they not had this 'mixed religion' experience. Is it possible, as some might contend, that they have not been exposed as fully as others in the intricacies of a particular tradition? Perhaps, though I would argue that, wherever they might land in terms of religious affiliation, they **are** coming from a background of good information regarding what constitutes religious differences.

It is not a bad thing at all to have a serious discussion about Catholic and Protestant differences. Looking at why Catholics pray for the dead and affirm Purgatory or the background behind mandatory celibacy for priests from a Catholic perspective is good for any sincere inquirer of any faith perspective to know. Likewise,

---

37 These include *Crossing the Street* as well as Robert LaRochelle, *What Roman Catholics Need to Know About Protestants* and *What Protestants Need to Know About Roman Catholics* (Gonzalez, Florida: Energion Publications).

being able to understand and articulate a Protestant counterpoint is, in my view, reflective of a strong religious education.

An argument against this would be that it is in a child's best interest to have an in depth grounding in the faith and practice of a particular tradition so as to be prepared to discuss it and compare it to others on solid ground. Some would argue that an inadequate grounding would lead to a susceptibility toward swaying with the wind when it comes to the effect of exposure upon belief. Another perspective would be that if one cannot understand another position from the point of view of that position then one's own is really a defensive posture in which one seeks to prove right one's own stance by refuting erroneous counterpoints. Within the Christian community, this catechetical approach has been quite popular for a long time, in Catholic, Protestant and Orthodox circles.[38] It is my contention that a catechism approach to religious education is inadequate in the current religious context. This is not to say that no place exists for learning from catechisms. Rather that the pedagogical approach has to be comparative and, most importantly, dialogical.[39]

My contention is that neither situation represents the ideal. In other words, it is not absolute fact that it is best to be raised by two Catholics or two Protestants, etc. In the same vein, there is likewise no disadvantage to being the child of two people committed to a common religious faith and practice. In the end, each individual must make religious choices based on her/his conscience, experience and use of human intelligence and reason. It is quite possible

---

38 Many traditions hold to a catechism which encapsulates the essence of the tradition's core beliefs. Knowledge of the contents of the catechism are essential. Such examples include *The Catechism of the Catholic Church, Luther's Small and Large Catechism, the Heidelberg Catechism, as well as many others.* Catholics of my generation were raised on *The Baltimore Catechism.* These books sum up the essential teachings of the faith in a question/answer format.

39 Significant shifts in religious education methodology has developed since the 1960's. This was reflected in the Christian Education materials published by organized religious groups.

that two people who truly love each other may have differing theological perspectives. When those exist, their exploration can be beneficial both to them as a couple and to those young people for whom they are responsible. My greatest concern, as I have stated in different ways, is when couples opt to take religion off the table as a topic for discussion, all too often out of fear that discussing it will be far too divisive.

In my view, the bottom line for **both** couples and children is that people engage, and are given the opportunity to engage, in significant discussion regarding the great questions of which we have spoken, these questions of our origin and our destiny and the possible meaning attached to this time we live upon this earth! In light of some recent data pointing to religious disinterest, I am concerned that these great questions may not be dealt with as deeply and profoundly as they ought.

QUESTIONS FOR DISCUSSION

1. How do **you** see the advantages/disadvantages attached to interreligious relationships and child rearing?

2. If this applies to your relationship, how do you suggest the two of you handle it?

3. The author makes clear in several places that he believes that couples need to discuss religion. Are there ever situations when you think it is best not to do so? Please explain.

CHAPTER SIX

SUGGESTIONS AND STRATEGIES

Contending as I do that a relationship and a family can flourish even when individuals see religious issues differently and that a home can be a united one even as differences exist, it is my intention in this chapter to explore some suggestions and strategies to help make this happen. If you, the reader, are in the kind of relationship I have been writing about, I encourage you to take these suggestions seriously and to explore them deeply. I also encourage you to discuss with your most significant other the value of each. If you are a leader in a religious congregation and deal with ecumenical and interfaith[40] couples, I hope you will find these suggestions and the questions I raise helpful to you as well as you seek to help individuals and couples work through these issues. If you are in love, want a happy future, and want to do the best for yourself and the one you love, I encourage you to grapple with these religious questions and explore them as part of your relationship with the one you love, whatever your individual background might be. With this in mind, please consider the following ideas I wish to place before you for consideration and, ultimately, conversation:

1. It is important to do everything you can to learn about your loved one's religious approach.

Ask questions of the other. Read about agnosticism or Catholicism or Mormonism or whatever that approach may be. Go to services at his/her church/house of worship if he/she attends or wants to do so. If your beloved was raised in a tradition and has not been at worship in a while and is rumbling about how much

---

40 If you are such a leader, I strongly suggest that you develop such programs and/or build upon the ones you are currently leading.

he or she might miss it, offer to attend with her/him. If the two of you are responsible for raising children, do everything you can to teach them about their parents' particular beliefs and practices. Fill them in on the celebrations in your family of origin as you were growing up — of how you experienced Passover or Ramadan or Christmas as a child or maybe what it was like to grow up in a primarily secular environment. Talk about what you liked, didn't like and maybe what you really wondered about![41]

2. If one is comfortable with a religious approach, do not abandon it in the name of being united.

While I have been serving for nearly fourteen years as a pastor in the United Church of Christ, serving churches in both the UCC and the Evangelical Lutheran Church in America (ELCA), my wife has remained a Roman Catholic. For most of those years, Catholicism has simply represented her theology and approach to religious practice far more than participation in the UCC would. This statement is not reflective of either Catholicism or that particular Protestant denomination. Rather it points out the importance of my wife engaging in identification with a church community whose faith and practice resonated with what she saw as important for her own spiritual life. What she has done is, as I see it, good practice for any of us.

To be honest, I think that, all too often, people make accommodations without being at a reasonable peace with what they're accommodating toward. It **is** quite possible to experience religious diversity in even the closest relationships without affecting the quality of that relationship. In order to make this happen, it takes a spirit of mutual respect born of the foundational position of a profound LOVE!

---

41 Again, I encourage you to consider using and building upon the conversation starters you will find in this book.

54

3. Where possible, find common worship opportunities.

Possibly attend classes together. In my view, this is an area to which churches, temples, and mosques should pay considerable attention. It is important that local congregations reach out to couples who come from different religious backgrounds, including those of those cited in survey data as claiming no religious affiliation. Those connected with religious institutions could learn a lot from the lived experience of those who really don't see themselves as religiously connected. If you are a leader in a congregation, ordained or non ordained, and you are reading this book, please consider what YOU as a community can offer couples in interreligious relationships. Think about what you are doing in the religious education of your children to inculcate understanding of and respect for a variety of religious expressions. Are there classes or discussion opportunities you should be offering? Think about that — and talk about it. As religious congregations work with middle school and high school youth, this serious exposure to religious diversity should be high on the educational agenda. If you are part of one of these relationships, consider advocating with leaders of a local congregation to make these opportunities possible!

4. If it is not possible to share worship together, find ways to be together that may involve contact with the religious community of your partner, where applicable.

Settle for some kind of level of participation in the partner's practice of faith and the activities of her/his faith community in ways that do not compromise your conscience. Let us say, for example, that you are Jewish and your partner is Christian, attendance at a church fair or carnival or sports event or an educational program will not put you in a situation where you are compromising important tenets of your faith. Conversely, a Christian celebrating Passover dinner is actually enhancing one's faith by doing what Jesus did himself! There may be all kinds of situations wherein experiencing the practice of another tradition could enhance one's own, especially, though not limited to, how individuals see prayer.

5. Where children are involved, do not leave religious questions and practice to one member of the couple, but thoroughly talk through every possible facet of the 'which way to raise children' issue.

Sadly, very sadly, in my experience, I have found too many men who think the religious upbringing of children is "the woman's job." This is truly unfortunate!

An overall theme which underlies each of these suggestions is that couples should not ignore realities. For a multiplicity of reasons, the world of religious practice and affiliation is filled with all kinds of potential areas for significant tension. In the name of 'keeping the peace', couples may lose opportunities to explore some of life's most significant questions together. Likewise, they may miss out unnecessarily on drawing strength from religious institutions and traditions. Sadly, all too often, one member in a relationship has carried the burden of taking care of the religious education of children.

Sadly, too many men have yielded this responsibility to the woman in the relationship, just as so many have done the same in terms of a child's education outside of the religious realm. This is not good at all, for a wide variety of reasons, including that of providing a healthy climate in which a child can explore questions of religion.

If you, the reader, are in a relationship where these religious differences exist, I urge you to talk together about these suggestions I have made. If you are a leader in a religious congregation, I encourage you to consider what **your** community of faith can do to reach out to couples in these situations and to examine how the ways in which you embrace religious diversity may truly augment your congregation's strengths.

SOME QUESTIONS FOR DISCUSSION

1. Why do so many couples ignore discussing religion?
2. The author sees ignoring religious questions as a problem. Do you agree? Disagree? Why?
3. Respond to this:

   'If you take the author of this book seriously, all you will be doing is sitting around and discussing theology. That is not real. There is a lot more to do with a couple's life! Marriage, for example, is not a seminary or college religion classroom. The guy has got to get real!'

CHAPTER SEVEN

A HOME UNITED

Something led you to pick up this book! Maybe you are a spouse or partner and you wish that you and your beloved could share the same religious practice. Maybe you see marriage in your future and are worried that religion could be a divisive force in your relationship. Perhaps you are uncomfortable with the way religion has already divided your family. It is possible that you are really stuck in trying to figure out what is best for your current or prospective children.

It is my hope that whatever led you to pick up this book, you have found some valuable ideas to consider within these pages. I also hope that you have, and will continue to, take the time to participate in the discussion exercises I have included within these pages. At the core of my expectations is that, even where you and your beloved simply cannot agree with one another's theology and or religious practice, you can nonetheless find and affirm ever more deeply the common ground that you share.

As I have implied and directly stated throughout this book, members of any 'couple,' however close they may be, nonetheless always remain individuals. This is a good thing, not a negative at all and it is a fact that must not be lost in this desire to be united. Consequently, no individual, however much in love, should be coerced into believing something he or she does not believe or directly engaging in religious practices that run contrary to his/her conscience. This is precisely along the same lines of any kind of coercion which could all too readily creep into a relationship.

Specifically, with respect to religion, I do **not** believe that, for example, in a marriage between a Christian and a Buddhist, even in a situation where as a couple a choice has been raised to raise children in the Christian tradition, there should be any expectation on the part of the Christian that the Buddhist will abandon aspects of her/his faith and practice in the name of unity. As a matter of fact, I would assert that in doing so, the Buddhist would not really be contributing to unity at all. That individual instead would be repressing a very important part of how she/he understands, conceptualizes and responds to reality.

It is a strong conviction of mine that, before God, one must act on one's conscience and be faithful to one's own personal spiritual quest. Asserting the primacy of conscience is born of an understanding that where two or three are gathered, there may not always be a clear unity between or among them. With this understanding in mind, we need to explore the expectations behind the premise that couples and families can function well relationally where such clear cut religious differences might exist.

Here is where we wade or plunge, really, into deep and dangerous waters. Quite frankly, whether this can work depends to a great extent on how we as individuals deal with the issue of the relative merit of religious views different from our own. In order to explore this as clearly as I can, I need to speak about myself:

I am a Christian. In my Christian faith, I believe in God and likewise hold the conviction that Jesus of Nazareth is the One whom I choose to follow. I will gladly and with conviction affirm the tenets of the Apostle's and Nicene Creeds.[42] I believe this because I would, in faith, contend that the death and resurrection of Jesus has had a definitive impact upon my life. As I have grown up and thought this through, I have been most pleased to assert that, as I see it, seeking to imitate Jesus is significant to me in terms of coming to terms with life's meaning and purpose.[43]

---

42 These are the affirmations of faith accepted by such creedal churches as Roman Catholics, Anglicans and Lutherans.

43 As a starting point for reflection on this, I highly recommend this book: James Carroll, *Christ Actually* (New York, Viking Penguin, 2014).

In varied Christian traditions, this is expressed differently. In the words of a traditional Creed Christian believers, such as I, are comfortable saying: 'For us and for our salvation, He came down from heaven.'[44] Without even touching the issue of how literally one might take this, the understanding within that doctrinal statement is that there **is** a powerful connection between Jesus and my well being, on this earth and beyond! In fact, Jesus not only offers my life meaning upon this earth, but in Jesus, there is a window to understanding something about the mysteries of origin and destiny as well. [45]

With this in mind, what might I think about the religious faith of those who do **not** share my own conviction about Jesus? There are those, and I do **not** count myself among them, who would say that the faith of those who do not 'believe in'[46] Jesus is somehow insufficient. In other words, in the Christian- Muslim example, they would argue that the claims Muslims might make about a prophet born hundreds of years after Jesus are extraneous and detract from the core of true religion which is the basic acceptance of Jesus as Lord and Savior. They would make that claim of **all** religious approaches which do not assert that salvation comes through faith in Jesus Christ.

In reality, what I am saying is that, within my own Christian faith community, there are many who would argue that, since, in their view, Christianity is the 'true religion', it is best that the non Christian in a relationship convert to Christianity. My approach is different and will be met with criticism by some of my fellow Christians, who happen to be in a more conservative Christian milieu. To be perfectly honest, I think that the underlying convic-

44 From The Nicene Creed

45 Here is where a reflection upon Chapter One of John's Gospel may be helpful. This Prologue to the Gospel explores how Jesus was present at the beginning and then in time comes to exist upon our earth. It is a beautiful, albeit complex piece of Christian Scripture.

46 Much of the missionary thrust in conservative Christianity is centered on converting people to the 'one way' that is Jesus.

tions of this book will be extremely difficult to swallow for those within the Christian faith who believe that the non–Christian partner should, first and foremost, be converted to Christianity. The approach I am advocating here does **not** downplay my Christian convictions. Instead, it places emphasis on the fact that it is **my** Christian conviction, made in the privacy of my soul before my God and, believing as I do, in the sacredness of the relationship between the divine and the human, I understand that for someone else's relationship with the divine to be meaningful, it must be a reflection of the honest conviction of one's own mind and heart.

I have had many conversations over the years with those who are fully convinced that, in some cases, people from two different 'religions' are in for great difficulty should they seek to unite in marriage or a long term commitment. There are those who would argue that it is not wise for a Jew and Christian, as example, to marry each other. While fully respecting the position on intermarriage among many Jews, a position I did not understand well as a seventeen year old kid, and without engaging in debate about the wisdom of intermarriage in this situation, I would contend that a Jew and a Christian can join together and experience a long term happy marriage without being unfaithful to their religious beliefs. I am assuming some readers would quarrel with me. Hence, the discussion questions!

Within certain Christian traditions, individuals will make the argument that it is best to have both people in a relationship share the same church tradition or denomination. They would say that there are all kinds of impediments present among Christian practices, intercommunion being high on that list.[47] As I have mentioned before, this was certainly the position within my native Roman Catholicism for a very long time. Many Protestants, likewise, continue to have an aversion toward intermarriage with practicing Catholics. Having lived within the Protestant tradition for nearly two decades

---

47 There exists within the modern church a variety of approaches on the issue of intercommunion. I address this in *Crossing the Street*.

now, I wish I could say that anti-Catholicism has been fully erased from Protestant culture, but I cannot![48]

In looking at the broadest possible questions posed by my basic premises, however, I must state that, as I see it, believing in Jesus, affirming faith in Jesus as Lord and Savior, does **not** mean that the only way **all** human beings can achieve eternal salvation is to profess the same faith that I profess. Realizing that if you, the reader, have not figured out my position before you got to this chapter, many of you may turn off what I say right about now, I wish to explain that, in my view, several operative principles apply in this case:

1. God alone is God. That short sentence contains a lot!
2. We human beings are limited in our knowledge of God. When push comes to shove, there is more that we don't know about God than what we do. To this point, the more fundamentalist believers in all religions would argue that I am off base. They would say that God has truly revealed Himself in the Scriptures of their faith or the experience of their founder or in the personal revelations God has made. [49]Radical extremists would really contend (and did) that God wanted them to fly planes into the Twin Towers on September 11, 2001!
3. God desires the good of all. There seems to be a consensus among the broad base of most religious traditions that God wants what is good for us, though we don't really know literally exactly how God 'wants.'
4. There are deep commonalities between the teachings of Jesus and the ethical teachings of other traditions, including that of those who do not profess faith in God. Jesus has inspired many great thinkers who were not 'traditional 'Christians', including, but most certainly not limited to Mahatma Gandhi.[50] And it

---

48 A perusal of the Internet corroborates my lived experience regarding anti-Catholicism.

49 This tendency is found in many different traditions.

50 Gandhi's interest in Jesus and his teachings were clear in his writings.

is no coincidence that the distinguished Christian preacher Rev. Dr. Martin Luther King, Jr. was influenced by Gandhi.

5. Both within and outside of Christianity, there are those who stray from the core understanding of God as professed by Christians, i.e. the **love** of God for God's creation, manifest in God's grace toward us and the way we, in turn, love God through loving one another.

It is with this final point that I wish to end my part of this book. I encourage you to talk with each other about the questions I pose below and then to go back and talk some more about what I have asked you to discuss in the chapters that went before. As I conclude these observations I have shared with you, I wish to leave you with this:

In the very act of being a committed couple, you, regardless of your religious affiliation or lack thereof … **you** are loving God. That is the faith with which I have come to this task of writing this book. Even if you do not accept my religious premise, I want you to think about committed **love**.[51] What does it entail?

There are certainly those who would read my words and say that my approach is starry eyed and simplistic. They might contend that I am serving up a generic approach to religion laden with a 'feel good' philosophy and very little backbone. In response to that critique, I would state something quite the opposite. In doing so, I would cite the words of the novelist Fyodor Dostoyevsky as interpreted by the great Catholic activist Dorothy Day, a woman whose very lifestyle represented a radical, sacrificial commitment to the poorest of the poor. Day quoted the Russian novelist's assertion that 'Compared to fantasy, love is a harsh and dreadful thing.' While

---

51 It is important to explore and discuss the interrelationship between the reality of God's love for us and what it means to love God. We think of I John 4:16: *'God is love and the one who abides in God abides in love and God abides in that person'.* Note: I have provided an inclusive language translation of this piece of Christian Scriptural writing. It is faithful to the intent of the original words.

that phrase itself might seem, well, harsh and dreadful, I have to say that I concur with it.

I will contend that the essence of **love** includes specific acts of the will that take one outside of the selfish realm, that entail sacrifice and even, as needed, the willingness to suffer for the one you love.[52] Think of couples you have admired and known: Wives and husbands who have comforted each other in illness and tragedy. Parents who have made immeasurable sacrifices for the health and well being of their kids. Think of these individuals who have inspired their beloved with how they have gone out of their way to serve others in God's needy world. I want you to think of these powerful examples, quite possibly among your circle of family and friends, and talk to each other about them, all the while drawing inspiration for the way you live your common life!

When I speak of **a Home United**, yes, I am speaking as a Christian, but I am also speaking in a pluralistic world wherein organized religion has often contributed to the very opposite of unity and love. I am asking you, the reader, to live lives of love with those to whom you are committed. I am saying this with the conviction I find in my Scripture that, in the very act of real **love**, the love I profess was made incarnate in Jesus, in that very act of loving those whom we can see, we are loving the God we more than likely might think we can't!

Lastly, for this book to be what it was intended, I hope and trust that it will not simply be read and placed on a shelf. **Please** discuss it, argue with some of my premises, if you are so inclined, share your thoughts about what is written here with the most significant in your life. May this be a source for you in potentially divisive relationships so that, whatever your background and whether you call yourself a believer or not, a loyal member of an organized religious group, or one of that ever-growing number of 'nones,' you may find yourself more deeply united than perhaps you ever thought possible!

52 We think of the suffering love of Jesus as understood by Christians.

QUESTIONS FOR REFLECTION

1. When push comes to shove, should someone seek to marry or commit oneself to a person with the same religious approach?

2. If you are a Christian, do you believe that the eternal salvation of all people depends on their act of accepting Christ as their Savior?

3. Looking again at a question we have explored throughout this book: Ideally, is it best for marriage if a person has the same view of religion as her/his spouse?

4. What do you think of the phrase the author likes so much: 'Compared to fantasy, love is a harsh and dreadful thing?' Does that represent an unappealing, negative view of love?

5. What would you tell the author about his book? Are there topics you wish he would have addressed? Say what they are and consider having a conversation about them.

APPENDIX

A GUIDE TO THE DIFFERENT RELIGIOUS APPROACHES

This is a brief overview of different religious approaches which are most common in contemporary human experience. While these descriptions do not encompass all possibilities, they are intended to provide a useful guide for those wishing to explore religious variations that may exist between those who have chosen to shape a life together:

RELIGIONS OF THE WEST

JUDAISM: Acknowledged to be the oldest organized religious group in the Western world, Judaism traces its roots back to Abram (Abraham) nearly two thousand years prior to the birth of Jesus. As with all religious bodies, Judaism contains considerable diversity. Contemporary Judaism includes different expressions based on theology and practice. These different expressions place emphasis on certain aspects of the historic tradition and the practice of faith in contemporary culture. The most commonly known are Reformed, Orthodox and Conservative Judaism.

In addition, as being Jewish is both an ethnic and religious designation, there are many who see themselves as 'secular Jews', i.e. they consider themselves Jewish based on cultural and historic identity rather than religious belief or practice. Judaism in the modern era has been deeply affected by the horrors of the Holocaust and the subsequent development of the nation of Israel. As a result of the obliteration of so many Jews at the hands of the Third Reich, many modern Jews, secular and religious, are deeply concerned about the need to maintain Jewish identity. This has significant impact in terms of interreligious relationships, marriage and the rearing of children..

CHRISTIANITY: Christianity, defined as the religious approach in which followers see Jesus as the individual whose teachings they choose to follow, has been a powerful political force in Western Civilization and through its missionary efforts has had considerable impact upon the entire world. In general terms, Christianity has three main branches: Roman Catholicism, Orthodox Christianity and Protestantism.

In order to understand Christianity, one has to recognize that each of the branches is marked by considerable diversity and differences within them. There are what we would call both liberal and conservative movements within each tradition as well as differences in practice based on both theology and ethnic culture.

ISLAM: This Western religion has emerged as a topic for much exploration over these past two decades. Unfortunately, as a result of the rise in terrorist activity within the Islamic (Muslim) tradition, many individuals have an incomplete knowledge of the roots and beliefs of this long standing faith, which dates its founding to the revelations to and insights of the prophet Muhammad (approx. 570 CE).

Judaism, Christianity and Islam see themselves as *monotheistic* religious approaches, i.e. they believe that there is but one 'God'.

RELIGIONS OF THE EAST

HINDUISM: Many people are surprised to learn that Hinduism, which evolved in the nation we know as India, is the oldest living religion in the world. Unlike monotheistic Western religion, Hinduism does not affirm a faith in 'one God.' Notions of reincarnation and Nirvana are associated with this tradition. It is from the Hindu approach to religious belief and practice that Buddhism developed.

BUDDHISM: This Eastern religion, developed in adherence to the great teacher Siddhartha Gautama who came to be known as the 'Buddha' ('the awakened one'), places great emphasis on meditation as a means to achieve 'the right way of living.' Buddhism deemphasized the notion of any divine being. It has had major impact over the past few decades within Western Civilization as it provides different means to find peace and calm in a frenzied world. Such movements as Transcendental Meditation which have many adherents in the West has roots in a Buddhist philosophy.

While these five categories represent major religious groupings, they are hardly all encompassing. As I have pointed out in this book, agnosticism and atheism are religious approaches held by a number of individuals. Atheists and agnostics come to their positions for a variety of reasons and don't necessarily agree with each other with respect to the reasons for their approach.

In addition, there is disagreement among many regarding where to include certain organized religious groupings. There are also certain groups, Scientologists come to mind, who seem to stand outside of the boundaries of these traditional categorizations. Nonetheless, it does seem fair to assert that, in looking at religious thought and practice throughout the world, one could categorize most individuals in the world as falling within the groupings identified in this Appendix, seeing themselves as Christians, Jews, Muslims, agnostics, atheists, Hindus or Buddhists. We can say this with a full awareness that, for a good number, their religious perspective cannot be explained by any of these terms.

In light of the issues discussed in this book, it is important that we all have a healthy recognition of the wide variety of existing religious expressions as we seek to understand the place of religion in the most important relationships in our lives. It would also be of value to all of us if we would seek to learn more about religious variety in a pluralistic world. It is clear that this variety most definitely has an impact upon how we might shape our relationships!

SUGGESTED READINGS

Campbell, David E. and Putnam, Robert D. *American Grace*. New York: Simon and Schuster, 2010.

Carroll, James. *Christ Actually*. New York: Viking Penguin, 2014.

Katz Miller, Susan. *Being Both: Embracing Two Religions in One Interfaith Family*. Boston: Beacon Press 2013.

LaRochelle, Robert R. *Crossing the Street*. Gonzalez, Florida: Energion Publications, 2012.

_____ *What Protestants Need to Know about Roman Catholics*. Gonzalez, Florida: Energion Publications, 2013.

_____ *What Roman Catholics Need to Know about Protestants*. Gonzalez, Florida: Energion Publications, 2014.

Matthews, Chris. *JFK: Elusive Hero*. New York: Simon and Schuster, 2011.

O'Brien, David. *The Renewal of American Catholicism*. New York: Paulist Press, 1972.

"Pew Research Center Religious Landscape Surveys 2008." http://religions.pewforum.org/.

Prothero, Stephen. *Religious Literacy*. San Francisco: Harper San Francisco, 2007.

Roof, Wade Clark, *Spiritual Marketplace*. Princeton: Princeton University Press, 1999.

Shea, William. *The Lion and the Lamb*. Oxford: Oxford Press, 2004.

ALSO FROM ENERGION PUBLICATIONS

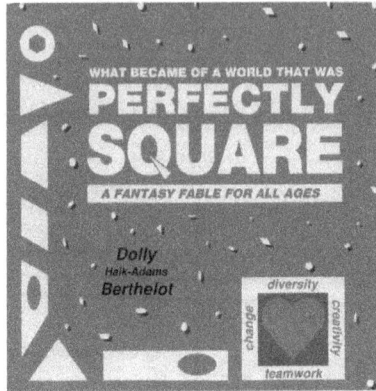

Perfectly Square is a charming, gentle little work that makes you smile and makes you think. The perception is beautiful. I just loved it.

Betty Williams
Nobel Peace Prize Winner, 1977

ALSO BY THE AUTHOR

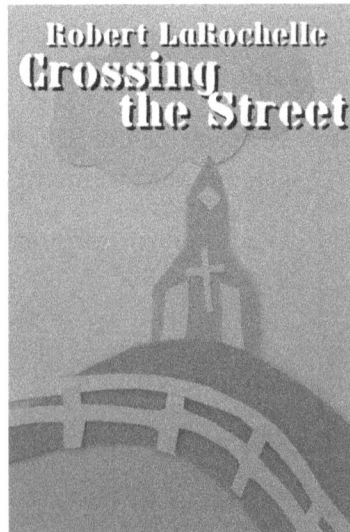

[Bob LaRochelle] makes a strong case for doing just that, crossing the street and finding out what our brothers and sisters are doing.

Susan Campbell
Columnist, *Hartford Courant*

More from Energion Publications

Personal Study

Finding My Way in Christianity	Herold Weiss	$16.99
The Sacred Journey	Chris Surber	$11.99

Christian Living

Faith in the Public Square	Robert D. Cornwall	$16.99
Grief: Finding the Candle of Light	Jody Neufeld	$8.99
Crossing the Street	Robert LaRochelle	$16.99
Life as Pilgrimage	David Moffett-Moore	14.99
What Protestants Need to Know about Roman Catholics	Robert LaRochelle	$4.99
What Roman Catholics Need to Know about Protestants	Robert LaRochelle	$4.99

Bible Study

Learning and Living Scripture	Lentz/Neufeld	$12.99
From Inspiration to Understanding	Edward W. H. Vick	$24.99
Philippians: A Participatory Study Guide	Bruce Epperly	$9.99
Ephesians: A Participatory Study Guide	Robert D. Cornwall	$9.99
Meditations on According to John	Herold Weiss	14.99

Theology

Creation in Scripture	Herold Weiss	$12.99
Creation: the Christian Doctrine	Edward W. H. Vick	$12.99
The Politics of Witness	Allan R. Bevere	$9.99
Ultimate Allegiance	Robert D. Cornwall	$9.99
The Journey to the Undiscovered Country	William Powell Tuck	$9.99
Process Theology	Bruce G. Epperly	$4.99

Ministry

Clergy Table Talk	Kent Ira Groff	$9.99
So Much Older Then …	Robert LaRochelle	$9.99

Generous Quantity Discounts Available
Dealer Inquiries Welcome
Energion Publications — P.O. Box 841
Gonzalez, FL 32560
Website: http://energionpubs.com
Phone: (850) 525-3916

www.ingramcontent.com/pod-product-compliance
Lightning Source LLC
Chambersburg PA
CBHW031605040426
42452CB00006B/420